Everlasting Love

By Cindy Mackenzie

Photography by my son, Bruce Mackenzie. These photographs were taken on his trip to Patagonia to raise money for St Andrews Hospice.

God speaks to you in many ways. Through His word as you read it, hearing it through Pastor's, Sunday School Teachers, Missionaries, and many more.

You can also see God through His creation of the world. These photographs captured by Bruce can help you to see His mighty handywork, through the world He made.

Dedication

I would like to dedicate this book to my parents. My Dad loved to play the organ and as he played the organ, we sang all the hymns. This gave me my first love of music. Music can be very moving and as I sang the words even as a young girl, I could feel God's presence in my life. These precious times helped to give me a good solid base to my faith in God.

My Mom was a great inspiration to me. She had a wonderful faith; and was a very practical woman. If someone was sick in the church, she made meals for them, she wrote letters, gave people lifts to church. She taught by example. She was a talented author as well. She wrote lovely poems and children's books.

As I look back, I realise now that my faith in God not only came from going to church and hearing God's word. It came from knowing God's word, believing it personally and living it out in practical ways. This came from my parents. Thank you, Mom and Dad.

TABLE OF CONTENTS

EVERLASTING LOVE

1 GIVE THANKS

REFLECTION:

As we reflect on this verse, we should take time to give thanks to God for all the blessings in our lives. Even in difficult times, we can find reasons to be grateful. We can thank God for our health, our families, our friends, and for the many opportunities He has given us to grow and learn.

When we focus on God's goodness and love, it can change our perspective and help us to approach life with gratitude and joy. It reminds us that we are not alone and that we have a loving God who cares for us and provides for our needs.

Let us take time today to give thanks to God for His goodness and love. May we be reminded of His faithfulness and may our hearts overflow with gratitude and praise.

DECLARATION:

Today, I declare that I will give thanks to the LORD for His goodness and unfailing love. I will not take for granted the many blessings in my life, but instead, I will pause to reflect on all the ways that God has shown me His love and faithfulness. I will have a heart of gratitude and acknowledge God as the source of all good things in my life.

MOTIVATION:

This verse reminds us that no matter what we are going through, God's goodness and love remain constant. Even in our darkest moments, we can find reasons to give thanks because God is always with us, guiding us, and providing for our needs.

PRAYER:

Dear God, thank You for Your goodness and love that endure forever. Help me to focus on Your faithfulness, even when I face difficulties and challenges in my life. May my heart overflow with gratitude, and may my life reflect Your love to those around me. In Jesus' name, I pray. Amen.

2 UNFAILING KINDNESS

SCRIPTURE

Jeremiah 31:3 says, "I have loved you with an everlasting love; I have drawn you with unfailing kindness."

REFLECTION:

This verse reminds us of the unfailing and everlasting love that God has for us. It is a love that never fades, no matter how much we may fail or stray from His path. It is a love that draws us back to Him, time and time again, with kindness and compassion.

DECLARATION:

Today, I declare that I am deeply loved by God. His love for me is unfailing and everlasting, and it will never run out. I declare that I will trust in His love, even when I feel unworthy or undeserving. I will rest in the knowledge that His love is enough to sustain me and guide me through every season of life.

MOTIVATION:

Knowing that God loves us with an everlasting love and unfailing kindness should motivate us to draw closer to Him. It should inspire us to live our lives in a way that honors Him and reflects His love to those around us. It should give us hope and courage to face whatever challenges may come our way, knowing that we are never alone.

PRAYER:

Heavenly Father, thank You for loving me with an everlasting love and unfailing kindness. Help me to trust in Your love and to draw closer to You each day. Give me the strength and courage to live my life in a way that honours You and reflects Your love to those around me. Thank You for Your faithfulness and goodness, and for drawing me back to You with Your love. Amen.

3 FAITHFUL GOD

SCRIPTURE

Deuteronomy 7:9. "Know therefore that the Lord your God is God; he is the faithful God, keeping his covenant of love to a thousand generations of those who love him and keep his commandments."

REFLECTION:

As we reflect on this verse, we are reminded of the importance of obedience to God's commands. When we obey God's commandments, we demonstrate our love for Him and open ourselves up to experience the fullness of His love and faithfulness.

Let us therefore strive to live a life that honours God and keeps His commandments. May we trust in His faithfulness and love, knowing that He is a God who keeps His promises to His people for generations to come.

As humans, we often struggle with being faithful to our commitments, and we may even break promises we've made to others. However, this verse reminds us that God is a faithful God who keeps His covenant and steadfast love with His people. He is always true to His promises and never fails us, even when we fall short.

DECLARATION:

Today, I declare that I will trust in the faithfulness of God. I will hold onto His promises and believe that He will keep His word. I will not doubt His love for me, but instead, I will lean on His steadfast love and find comfort in it.

MOTIVATION:

Knowing that God is a faithful God who keeps His covenant and steadfast love should motivate us to be faithful to Him. We should strive to live a life that pleases Him and keeps His commandments. As we walk in obedience, we can trust that God will be faithful to bless us and keep His promises to us.

PRAYER:

Dear God, thank You for Your faithfulness and steadfast love. Help me to trust in Your promises and to be faithful to You. Strengthen me to walk in obedience and to live a life that honours You. I pray that You would continue to keep Your covenant and steadfast love with me, and with generations to come. In Jesus' name, Amen.

4 EVERLASTING GOD

"

SCRIPTURE

Jeremiah 31:3 "I have loved you with an everlasting love; I have drawn you with unfailing kindness."

REFLECTION:

This verse reminds us of the incredible depth and constancy of God's love for us. His love is not temporary or fleeting, but everlasting. He loved us before we even knew Him and will continue to love us for all eternity. This love is not based on anything we have done or can do but is a pure expression of God's character and nature.

DECLARATION:

Today, I declare that I am loved with an everlasting love by God. I am secure in His love, and nothing can separate me from it. I will rest in the knowledge that His love for me is unchanging, unconditional, and unfailing.

MOTIVATION:

Knowing that we are loved with an everlasting love can motivate us to live a life that honours and glorifies God. We can respond to His love by loving others, serving Him with our whole hearts, and sharing His love with those around us. We can also find comfort and strength in His love during times of trial and hardship, knowing that He is always with us and will never leave us.

PRAYER:

Heavenly Father, thank You for loving me with an everlasting love. Help me to truly grasp the depth of Your love for me and to respond to it with a life of love, obedience, and service. May Your love motivate me to love others as You have loved me and to be a shining light for Your kingdom. In Jesus' name, Amen.

5 GOD IS LOVE

REFLECTION:

The phrase "God is love" is one of the most profound and powerful statements in all of scripture. It captures the very essence of who God is and what He desires for us as His children. In 1 John 4:16-18, we are reminded that this love that God has for us is not based on anything we have done or will do, but God gives us this gift that He offers to us out of His own character.

DECLARATION:

I declare that God's love for me is steadfast and unchanging. I will not be afraid or anxious, because His love casts out fear. I trust in His perfect love, which was demonstrated through the sacrifice of Jesus on the cross.

MOTIVATION:

Knowing that God is love and that His love is perfect, I am motivated to love others in the same way. I desire to extend grace, forgiveness, and kindness to those around me, just as God has done for me. I will seek to love even those who are difficult to love, knowing that God's love is greater than any obstacle or challenge.

PRAYER:

Dear God, I thank You for the gift of Your love. Help me to fully grasp the depth and breadth of Your love for me, and to live each day in the confidence of Your steadfast love. Empower me to love others with the same selfless love that You have shown to me, and to be a vessel of Your love to those who are hurting or in need. In Jesus' name, Amen.

6 ABIDE IN HIS LOVE

SCRIPTURE

John 15:9-10: "As the Father has loved me, so have I loved you. Now remain in my love. If you keep my commands, you will remain in my love, just as I have kept my Father's commands and remain in his love."

REFLECTION:

In John 15:9-10, Jesus invites us to abide in His love. This is a call to remain connected to Him, to make our home in His love, and to live our lives from a place of deep intimacy with Him. When we abide in His love, we experience the fullness of His joy and our lives bear fruit that glorifies God.

DECLARATION:

I declare that I will abide in the love of Jesus. I will remain connected to Him and make my home in His love. I will trust in His love for me, even when I don't understand His ways, and I will live my life from a place of deep intimacy with Him.

MOTIVATION:

Knowing that Jesus loves me and desires for me to abide in His love motivates me to pursue a life of surrender and obedience to Him. I want to experience the fullness of His joy and bear fruit that glorifies God. I am motivated to remain connected to Him, even during difficult circumstances, because I know that His love is steadfast and unchanging.

PRAYER:

Dear Jesus, I thank You for Your love for me. Help me to abide in Your love, to make my home in it, and to live my life from a place of deep intimacy with You. Give me the strength to remain connected to You, on daily basis, and to trust in Your love for me. May my life bear fruit that glorifies

God and brings You honor and praise. In your name I pray, Amen.

7 GOD IS WITH YOU

Zephaniah 3:17 "The Lord your God is with you, the Mighty Warrior who saves. He will take great delight in you; in his love he will no longer rebuke you but will rejoice over you with singing."

REFLECTION:

Zephaniah 3:17 is a powerful reminder that God is always with us, no matter what we are going through. He is present in our joys and our sorrows, and He takes delight in us. This verse speaks to the love and care that God has for His people, and the comfort that comes from knowing that He is always by our side.

DECLARATION:

I declare that the Lord my God is with me always. He is my constant companion and my source of strength. I will not be afraid, for He is with me. I will trust in His love and care for me, even when life is difficult.

MOTIVATION:

Knowing that God is with me, no matter what, gives me the motivation to keep going, even when I feel like giving up. I am encouraged by the fact that He takes delight in me, and that He rejoices over me with singing. This motivates me to live my life for His glory, and to share His love with others.

PRAYER:

Dear God, thank You for Your constant presence in my life. Help me to trust in Your love and care for me, even when I don't understand what You are doing. Give me the strength to keep going, even when life is difficult, and the courage to share Your love with those around me. May my life bring You honour and glory, and may I always remember that You are with me. In Jesus' name, Amen.

8 MORE THAN CONQUERORS

"

SCRIPTURE

Romans 8:37-39 "No, in all these things we are more than conquerors through him who loved us. For I am convinced that neither death nor life, neither angels nor demons, neither the present nor the future, nor any powers, neither height nor depth, nor anything else in all creation, will be able to separate us from the love of God that is in Christ Jesus our Lord."

REFLECTION:

Romans 8:37-39 is a powerful reminder of the unfailing love of God for His children. We are more than conquerors through Christ who loved us, and nothing can separate us from His love. This passage speaks to the power and victory that we have in Christ, no matter what our circumstances.

DECLARATION:

I declare that I am more than a conqueror through Christ who loved me. I will not be defeated by the trials of life, for God is with me and His love sustains me. I will trust in His unfailing love for me, even when I don't understand His ways.

MOTIVATION:

Knowing that I am more than a conqueror through Christ motivates me to live my life with courage and confidence. I am encouraged by the fact that nothing can separate me from the love of God, and that His love gives me the strength to face any challenge that comes my way.

PRAYER:

Dear God, thank You for Your unfailing love for me. Help me to remember that I am more than a conqueror through Christ, and that nothing can separate me from Your love. Give me the strength to face any challenge that comes my way, and the courage to trust in Your love for me. May my life bring You glory and honour, and may I always remember the victory that I have in Christ. In Jesus' name, Amen.

9 WHAT GREAT LOVE

"

SCRIPTURE

1 John 3:1 *"See what great love the Father has lavished on us, that we should be called children of God!"*

REFLECTION:

1 John 3:1 reminds us of the incredible love that God has for us as His children. He calls us His own, and His love for us is beyond measure. This verse invites us to reflect on the greatness of God's love, and to embrace our identity as His beloved children.

DECLARATION:

I declare that I am a child of God, and that I am loved by Him with a great love. I will live my life from a place of confidence and security in His love for me. I will embrace my identity as His beloved child, and I will seek to reflect His love to others.

MOTIVATION:

The knowledge that I am loved by God with a great love motivates me to live my life with purpose and passion. I am encouraged by the fact that God has called me His own, and that He has a plan for my life. His love gives me the strength to face any challenge that comes my way.

PRAYER:

Dear God, thank You for Your great love for me. Help me to see myself as Your beloved child, and to live my life from a place of confidence and security in Your love for me. Give me the strength to face any challenge that comes my way, and the courage to reflect Your love to those around me. May my life bring You glory and honour, and may I always remember the greatness of Your love. In Jesus' name, Amen.

10 HUMBLE YOURSELVES

"

SCRIPTURE

1 Peter 5:6-7 "Humble yourselves, therefore, under God's mighty hand, that he may lift you up in due time. Cast all your anxiety on him because he cares for you."

REFLECTION:

1 Peter 5:6-7 reminds us to humble ourselves before God, recognising that He is in control of all things. We are called to cast all our anxieties on Him, knowing that He cares for us. This passage speaks to the peace and rest that comes from surrendering our worries to God and trusting in His loving care for us.

DECLARATION:

I declare that I will humble myself before God, recognising that He is in control of all things. I will cast all my anxieties on Him, knowing that He cares for me. I will trust in His loving care for me, even when I don't understand His ways.

MOTIVATION:

Knowing that I can cast all my anxieties on God and trust in His loving care for me, motivates me to live my life with peace and rest. I am encouraged by the fact that God cares for me, and that He is always with me, even during difficult circumstances.

PRAYER:

Dear God, thank You for Your loving care for me. Help me to humble myself before You, recognising that You are in control of all things. Give me the strength to cast all my anxieties on You, and to trust in Your loving care for me. May my life bring You honour and glory, and may I always remember the peace and rest that comes from surrendering my worries to You. In Jesus' name, Amen.

11 HE FIRST LOVED US

SCRIPTURE

1 John 4:19 "We love because he first loved us."

REFLECTION:

1 John 4:19 reminds us that our ability to love others is rooted in the fact that God first loved us. His love for us is the source of our love for others, and it is only through His love that we can truly love others as we ought. This passage invites us to reflect on the love that God has shown us, and to allow that love to flow out to those around us.

DECLARATION:

I declare that I will love others because God first loved me. I will allow His love to flow through me and into the lives of those around me. I will seek to reflect His love to others in all that I do.

MOTIVATION:

Knowing that my ability to love others is rooted in God's love for me motivates me to live my life with compassion and kindness. I am encouraged by the fact that God loves me unconditionally, and that He has called me to love others in the same way.

PRAYER:

Dear God, thank You for loving me first. Help me to love others as You have loved me. May Your love flow through me and into the lives of those around me. Give me the strength to reflect Your love to others in all that I do. May my life bring You honour and glory, and may others see Your love through me. In Jesus' name, Amen.

12 LOVE EACH OTHER DEEPLY

SCRIPTURE

1 Peter 4:8 "Above all, love each other deeply, because love covers a multitude of sins."

REFLECTION:

1 Peter 4:8 encourages us to love one another deeply, recognising that love covers a multitude of sins. This verse reminds us that love is the foundation of our relationships with others, and that it is through love that we can show grace and forgiveness to those around us.

DECLARATION:

I declare that I will love others deeply, recognising that love covers a multitude of sins. I will seek to build strong and meaningful relationships with those around me and will extend grace and forgiveness to others through my love.

MOTIVATION:

The knowledge that loves covers a multitude of sins motivates me to live my life with compassion and forgiveness towards others. I am encouraged by the fact that love is the foundation of my relationships with others, and that it is through love that I can make a difference in the lives of those around me.

PRAYER:

Dear God, thank You for Your love for me. Help me to love others deeply, recognising that love covers a multitude of sins. May my relationships with others be built on a foundation of love, and may I extend grace and forgiveness to those around me through my love. Give me the strength to reflect Your love to others in all that I do. In Jesus' name, Amen.

13 DO EVERYTHING IN LOVE

SCRIPTURE

1 Corinthians 16:14 "Do everything in love."

REFLECTION:

1 Corinthians 16:14 reminds us that love should be the motivation behind everything that we do. Whether it is serving others, sharing the gospel, or simply going about our daily tasks, we are called to

do so with a spirit of love. This verse invites us to reflect on the importance of love in our lives, and to make it the driving force behind all that we do.

DECLARATION:

I declare that I will let all that I do be done in love. I will seek to live my life with a spirit of love, whether it is in serving others, sharing the gospel, or simply going about my daily tasks. I will make love the driving force behind all that I do.

MOTIVATION:

The knowledge that love should be the motivation behind everything that we do motivates me to live my life with compassion and kindness towards others. I am encouraged by the fact that when we love others, we reflect the love of Christ to them, and can make a difference in their lives.

PRAYER:

Dear God, thank You for Your love for me. Help me to let all that I do be done in love. May I live my life with a spirit of love, whether it is in serving others, sharing the gospel, or simply going about my daily tasks. Give me the strength to reflect Your love to others in all that I do. May my life bring You honour and glory, and may others see Your love through me. In Jesus' name, Amen.

14 ABOVE ALL PUT ON LOVE

REFLECTION:

Colossians 3:14 encourages us to put on love above all things, recognising that love binds everything together in perfect harmony. This verse reminds us that love is the foundation of our relationships with others, and that it is through love that we can show compassion, forgiveness, and grace to those around us.

DECLARATION:

I declare that I will put on love above all things. I will seek to live my life with a spirit of love, recognising that it is through love that I can show compassion, forgiveness, and grace to those around me. I will make love the foundation of my relationships with others.

MOTIVATION:

The knowledge that love is the foundation of our relationships with others motivates me to live my life with compassion and kindness towards others. I am encouraged by the fact that love is the key to showing grace and forgiveness, and that it is through love that we can make a difference in the lives of those around us.

PRAYER:

Dear God, thank You for Your love for me. Help me to put on love above all things. May I live my life with a spirit of love, recognising that it is through love that I can show compassion, forgiveness, and grace to those around me. Give me the strength to reflect Your love to others in all that I do. May my life bring You honour and glory, and may others see Your love through me. In Jesus' name, Amen.

15 BE HUMBLE AND GENTLE

SCRIPTURE

Ephesians 4:2-3 "Be completely humble and gentle; be patient, bearing with one another in love. Make every effort to keep the unity of the Spirit through the bond of peace."

REFLECTION:

Ephesians 4:2-3 encourages us to live our lives with humility, gentleness, patience, and love. These virtues are key to maintaining unity and peace within the body of Christ. This passage reminds us that our attitude towards others should be marked by humility, gentleness, patience, and love, as we strive to keep the bond of peace between us.

DECLARATION:

I declare that I will live my life with humility, gentleness, patience, and love. I will seek to maintain unity and peace within the body of Christ by having a heart of humility towards others, being gentle in my words and actions, having patience in difficult situations, and showing love to all those I encounter.

MOTIVATION:

The knowledge that humility, gentleness, patience, and love are key to maintaining unity and peace within the body of Christ motivates me to live my life with these virtues in mind. I am encouraged by the fact that when we practice these virtues, we reflect the character of Christ to those around us and can make a difference in their lives.

PRAYER:

Dear God, thank You for Your love for me. Help me to live my life with humility, gentleness, patience, and love. May I maintain unity and peace within the body of Christ by having a heart of humility towards others, being gentle in my words and actions, having patience in difficult situations, and showing love to all those I encounter. Give me the strength to reflect Your character to others in all that I do. May my life bring You honour and glory, and may others see Your love through me. In Jesus' name, Amen.

16 GOD COMMANDS US TO LOVE

"

SCRIPTURE

1 John 4:21 "And he has given us this command: Anyone who loves God must also love their brother and sister."

REFLECTION:

1 John 4:21 reminds us that the commandment to love God and love our fellow believers is not optional, but essential to our faith. This verse tells us that if we don't love our brother, whom we have seen, how can we love God, whom we have not seen? This passage reminds us that loving others is an expression of our love for God, and that we cannot separate the two.

DECLARATION:

I declare that I will follow the commandment to love God and love my fellow believers. I will seek to love others as an expression of my love for God, recognising that I cannot separate the two. I will strive to show love to all those I encounter, including those who are difficult to love.

MOTIVATION:

The knowledge that loving others is an expression of our love for God motivates me to follow the commandment to love. I am encouraged by the fact that when we show love to others, we reflect the character of Christ to those around us and can make a difference in their lives.

PRAYER:

Dear God, thank You for Your love for me. Help me to follow the commandment to love You and love my fellow believers. May I love others as an expression of my love for You, recognising that I cannot separate the two. Give me the strength to show love to all those I encounter, even those who are difficult to love. May my life bring You honour and glory, and may others see Your love through me. In Jesus' name, Amen.

17 LOVE YOUR ENEMIES

"

SCRIPTURE

Luke 6:35 "But love your enemies, do good to them, and lend to them without expecting to get anything back. Then your reward will be great, and you will be children of the Most High, because he is kind to the ungrateful and wicked."

REFLECTION:

Luke 6:35 challenges us to love our enemies and do good to those who hate us. This is a difficult task, but it is what sets us apart as followers of Christ. When we choose to love our enemies, we show that we are living according to a higher standard than the world around us. This passage reminds us that God's love is not limited to those who love Him back but extends even to those who are our enemies.

DECLARATION:

I declare that I will love my enemies and do good to those who hate me. I will choose to live according to a higher standard than the world around me, by extending love to those who may not deserve it. I will strive to see others through the eyes of Christ, recognising that they too are made in the image of God.

MOTIVATION:

The knowledge that God's love extends even to our enemies motivates me to love those who may be difficult to love. I am encouraged by the fact that when we choose to love our enemies, we reflect the character of Christ to those around us and can make a difference in their lives.

PRAYER:

Dear God, thank You for Your love for me, even when I was Your enemy. Help me to love my enemies and do good to those who hate me. Give me the strength to live according to a higher standard than the world around me, by extending love to those who may not deserve it. Help me to see others through the eyes of Christ, recognising that they too are made in Your image. May my life bring You honour and glory, and may others see Your love through me. In Jesus' name, Amen.

18 FAITHFUL GOD

SCRIPTURE

Deuteronomy 7:9 " Know therefore that the Lord your God is God; he is the faithful God, keeping his covenant of love to a thousand generations of those who love him and keep his commandments."

REFLECTION:

As we reflect on this verse, we are reminded of the importance of obedience to God's commands. When we obey God's commandments, we demonstrate our love for Him and open ourselves up to experience the fullness of His love and faithfulness.

Let us therefore strive to live a life that honours God and keeps His commandments. May we trust in His faithfulness and love, knowing that He is a God who keeps His promises to His people for generations to come.

As humans, we often struggle with being faithful to our commitments, and we may even break promises we've made to others. However, this verse reminds us that God is a faithful God who keeps His covenant and steadfast love with His people. He is always true to His promises and never fails us, even when we fall short.

DECLARATION:

Today, I declare that I will trust in the faithfulness of God. I will hold onto His promises and believe that He will keep His word. I will not doubt His love for me, but instead, I will lean on His steadfast love and find comfort in it.

MOTIVATION:

Knowing that God is a faithful God who keeps His covenant and steadfast love should motivate us to be faithful to Him. We should strive to live a life that pleases Him and keeps His commandments. As we walk in obedience, we can trust that God will be faithful to bless us and keep His promises to us.

PRAYER:

Dear God, thank you for your faithfulness and steadfast love. Help me to trust in your promises and to be faithful to you. Strengthen me to walk in obedience and to live a life that honours you. I pray that you would continue to keep your covenant and steadfast love with me, and with generations to come. In Jesus' name, Amen.

19 DO GOOD TO THOSE THAT HATE YOU

SCRIPTURE

Luke 6:27-31 "But to you who are listening I say: Love your enemies, do good to those who hate you, bless those who curse you, pray for those who mistreat you. If someone slaps you on one cheek, turn to them the other also. If someone takes your coat, do not withhold your shirt from them. Give to everyone who asks you, and if anyone takes what belongs to you, do not demand it back. Do to others as you would have them do to you."

REFLECTION:

Luke 6:27-31 challenges us to love our enemies, do good to those who hate us, bless those who curse us, and pray for those who mistreat us. This is not the natural response of our flesh, but it is what sets us apart as followers of Christ. This passage reminds us that God's love is not limited to those who love Him back but extends even to those who are our enemies. When we choose to love our enemies, we reflect the character of Christ to those around us.

DECLARATION:

I declare that I will love my enemies, do good to those who hate me, bless those who curse me, and pray for those who mistreat me. I will choose to live according to the teaching of Christ, even when it is difficult. I will strive to see others through the eyes of Christ, recognising that they too are made in the image of God.

MOTIVATION:

The knowledge that God's love extends even to our enemies motivates me to love those who may be difficult to love. I am encouraged by the fact that when we choose to love our enemies, we reflect the character of Christ to those around us and can make a difference in their lives. I am also motivated by the promise that when we give, it will be given back to us, pressed down, shaken together, and running over.

PRAYER:

Dear God, thank you for your love for me, even when I was your enemy. Help me to love my enemies, do good to those who hate me, bless those who curse me, and pray for those who mistreat me. Give me the strength to live according to the teaching of Christ, even when it is difficult. Help me to see others through the eyes of Christ, recognising that they too are made in your image. May my life bring you honour and glory, and may others see your love through me. In Jesus' name, Amen.

20 LOVE NEVER FAILS

"

SCRIPTURE

1 Corinthians 13:4-8" Love is patient, love is kind. It does not envy, it does not boast, it is not proud. It does not dishonour others, it is not self-seeking, it is not easily angered, it keeps no record of wrongs. Love does not delight in evil but rejoices with the truth. It always protects, always trusts, always hopes, always perseveres. Love never fails. But where there are prophecies, they will cease; where there are tongues, they will be stilled; where there is knowledge, it will pass away."

REFLECTION:

In these verses, Paul gives us a beautiful description of love - patient, kind, not envious, not proud, not rude, not self-seeking, not easily angered, keeps no record of wrongs, does not delight in evil but rejoices with the truth, always protects, always trusts, always hopes, always perseveres. This is the kind of love that God has for us, and the kind of love that we are called to have for others.

DECLARATION:

Today, I declare that I will strive to show this kind of love to those around me. I will be patient and kind, even when it's difficult. I will not be envious or proud but will instead focus on others and their needs. I will not be rude or self-seeking but will seek to serve others. I will not be easily angered or keep a record of wrongs but will forgive and let go of any bitterness. I will rejoice in the truth and seek to protect, trust, hope, and persevere in all things.

MOTIVATION:

The motivation for this kind of love is the love that God has shown us. He loved us so much that He sent His Son to die for us, and He continues to love us even when we fail Him. We are called to love others in the same way, with a sacrificial and selfless love that puts others before ourselves.

PRAYER:

Dear God, thank you for showing us what true love looks like. Help us to love others in the same way that you have loved us - with patience, kindness, and selflessness. Help us to let go of any bitterness or anger and to forgive others as you have forgiven us. Give us the strength and motivation to love others sacrificially, even when it's difficult. We pray this in Jesus' name, Amen.

21 TWO ARE BETTER THAN ONE

SCRIPTURE

Ecclesiastes 4:9-12 "Two are better than one, because they have a good return for their labour."

REFLECTION:

The author of Ecclesiastes writes about the value of companionship and teamwork. He emphasises that two people working together can achieve much more than a single individual working alone. The passage highlights the importance of having someone to share our joys and sorrows with, someone to lean on in difficult times, and someone to celebrate our victories with.

DECLARATION:

As we go through life, we may be tempted to go it alone, believing that we can handle everything on our own. However, the truth is that we need other people in our lives. We need friends, family, and loved ones who can offer support, encouragement, and guidance when we need it most.

MOTIVATION:

This passage should motivate us to seek out meaningful relationships and to invest in those relationships. We should be intentional about cultivating friendships, building community, and being there for others when they need us. By doing so, we not only enrich our own lives but also contribute to the greater good.

PRAYER:

Dear God, thank you for the people in our lives who bring us joy, comfort, and support. Help us to cherish those relationships and to be intentional about investing in them. Give us the strength to be there for others when they need us and to seek out help when we need it ourselves. May we always remember that two are better than one and that we are stronger together than we are alone. Amen.

22 HUSBANDS LOVE YOUR WIVES

REFLECTION:

I declare that as a husband, I will love my wife sacrificially, just as Christ loved the church and gave Himself up for her. I will prioritise her needs above my own and seek to serve her in all areas of our marriage. I will seek to understand and honour her, and to communicate with her in a way that demonstrates love and respect. I will be faithful and committed to her and will work to build a strong and lasting marriage that glorifies God.

DECLARATION :

As a husband, I declare that I will strive to love my wife with the same sacrificial love that Christ has for the Church. I will put her needs and desires before my own and seek to serve her in all things.

MOTIVATION:

The motivation to love my wife sacrificially comes from the knowledge that this is how Christ loved the church and demonstrated His love for us. I am motivated by the desire to honor God in my marriage, and to reflect His love and faithfulness in the way I love and serve my wife. Additionally, the knowledge that sacrificial love leads to a strong and lasting marriage motivates me to prioritise my wife's needs above my own.

PRAYER:

Dear God, thank you for the gift of marriage and for the example of Christ's sacrificial love. Help me to love my wife in the same way, giving myself up for her and prioritising her needs above my own. Give me the strength to serve her selflessly and to communicate with her in a way that honours and respects her. May our marriage reflect your love and faithfulness, and may we work together to build a strong and lasting union that glorifies you. In Jesus' name, Amen.

23 ONE FLESH

REFLECTION:

Genesis 2:24 states, "Therefore a man shall leave his father and his mother and hold fast to his wife, and they shall become one flesh." This verse describes the divine design for marriage as a sacred union between a man and a woman, intended for a lifetime commitment. The phrase "one flesh" refers to the physical and spiritual intimacy that is created through the union of marriage. This intimate bond is meant to be cherished and protected and serves as a reflection of the relationship between Christ and the church.

DECLARATION:

I declare that I will honour and respect the sanctity of marriage as God has designed it. I will hold fast to my spouse, cherishing and protecting the intimate bond that we share. I will strive to be selfless, putting the needs of my spouse before my own. I will seek to glorify God through my marriage, and to model the sacrificial love that Christ has for His church.

MOTIVATION:

The motivation to honour the sanctity of marriage and to cherish the intimate bond with my spouse comes from the knowledge that this union reflects the relationship between Christ and the church. Just as Christ sacrificially gave Himself for the church, I am called to sacrificially love and serve my spouse. Additionally, the commitment to my spouse is strengthened by the promise that God will be with us and bless our marriage as we honour Him.

PRAYER:

Dear God, thank you for the gift of marriage and for designing it as a sacred union between a man and a woman. Help me to honour and respect the sanctity of marriage, holding fast to my spouse and cherishing the intimate bond that we share. Help me to be selfless, putting the needs of my spouse before my own, and to seek to glorify You through my marriage. May You be at the center of our relationship, and may our marriage reflect the relationship between Christ and the church. In Jesus' name, Amen.

24 LET NO ONE SEPARATE

"

SCRIPTURE

Mark 10:9 "Therefore what God has joined together, let no one separate".

REFLECTION:

Mark 10:9 states, "Therefore what God has joined together, let no one separate." This verse speaks to the sanctity of marriage as a divine union, designed and ordained by God. It emphasises the commitment and covenant nature of marriage, and the importance of honouring that commitment for a lifetime. The phrase "let no one separate" is a powerful reminder that marriage is not to be taken lightly, and that the union between two people is meant to be permanent.

DECLARATION:

I declare that I will honour and respect the sanctity of marriage as a divine union designed by God. I will seek to strengthen and protect my marriage, committing myself to my spouse for a lifetime. I will not allow anything to come between us, and I will not consider divorce as an option. I will trust in God's design for marriage, and I will work to cultivate a loving, fulfilling relationship with my spouse.

MOTIVATION:

The motivation to honor and respect the sanctity of marriage comes from the knowledge that this union is designed by God and intended to reflect His love and faithfulness. Additionally, the commitment to my spouse is strengthened by the promise that God will be with us and bless our marriage as we honour Him. I am motivated by the desire to cultivate a deep and lasting relationship with my spouse, and to model the love of Christ in our marriage.

PRAYER:

Dear God, thank you for designing marriage as a divine union between a man and a woman. Help me to honour and respect the sanctity of marriage, committing myself to my spouse for a lifetime. I pray that you would strengthen and protect our marriage, and that we would never consider separation or divorce. Help us to trust in your design for marriage, and to cultivate a loving, fulfilling relationship that honours you. May our marriage reflect your love and faithfulness, and may we always seek to honour and glorify you. In Jesus' name, Amen.

25 WHAT DOES GOD REQUIRE OF US?

SCRIPTURE

Micah 6:8 "He has shown you, O mortal, what is good. And what does the Lord require of you? To act justly and to love mercy and to walk humbly with your God."

REFLECTION:

Micah 6:8 is a powerful reminder of what it means to live a life that is pleasing to God. The verse outlines three key principles that should guide our actions: acting justly, loving mercy, and walking humbly with God. This means that we are to be people who stand up for what is right, who show compassion and kindness to others, and who maintain a posture of humility before God. It's not enough to simply believe in God; we must live out our faith in tangible ways that reflect His character and values.

DECLARATION:

I declare that I will seek to live a life that is pleasing to God by acting justly, loving mercy, and walking humbly with Him. I will stand up for what is right, even when it is difficult or unpopular. I will show compassion and kindness to those around me, extending mercy and grace as I have received from God. I will maintain a posture of humility before God, recognising my need for Him in every area of my life.

MOTIVATION:

The motivation to live a life that is pleasing to God comes from a desire to honour Him and to reflect His character and values. We are called to be people who make a positive difference in the world, standing up for justice and showing love and compassion to those around us. As we walk humbly with God, we are empowered to live out our faith in tangible ways that impact the world for good.

PRAYER:

Dear God, thank you for the reminder that you require us to act justly, love mercy, and walk humbly with you. Help me to live out these principles in my daily life, standing up for what is right, showing compassion and kindness to others, and maintaining a posture of humility before you. Give me the strength and courage to make a positive difference in the world, and to reflect your character and values in all that I do. May my life be a pleasing offering to you. In Jesus' name, Amen.

26 THE NEEDY

SCRIPTURE

Psalm 9:18 *"But God will never forget the needy; the hope of the afflicted will never perish."*

REFLECTION:

Psalm 9:18 reminds us that God is aware of the needs of the needy and vulnerable, and that He will not forget them. This verse speaks to God's justice and compassion, and His promise to intervene on behalf of those who are in need. It is a powerful reminder that no one is forgotten or overlooked by God, and that He sees and cares for the oppressed and downtrodden.

DECLARATION:

I declare that I will trust in God's justice and compassion, and I will not forget the needs of the needy around me. I will seek to be a voice for those who are oppressed and vulnerable, and I will work to support and uplift those who are in need. I will trust in God's promise that the needy will not always be forgotten, and I will have faith that He will intervene on their behalf.

MOTIVATION:

The motivation to remember and care for the needs of the needy comes from the knowledge that every person is made in God's image and is deserving of dignity and respect. Additionally, the promise of Psalm 9:18 reminds us that God is actively involved in the lives of the vulnerable and oppressed, and that He invites us to join Him in His work of justice and compassion.

PRAYER:

Dear God, thank You for Your justice and compassion, and for Your promise that the needy will not be forgotten. Help me to remember and care for the needs of those around me, and to be a voice for the oppressed and vulnerable. I pray that You would intervene on their behalf, and that You would bring healing and hope to those who are in need. May I be an instrument of Your love and compassion in the world and may Your justice and mercy reign. In Jesus' name, Amen.

27 FOLLOW GOD'S EXAMPLE

SCRIPTURE

Matthew 25:35-40 "For I was hungry, and you gave me something to eat, I was thirsty, and you gave me something to drink, I was a stranger and you invited me in, I needed clothes, and you clothed me, I was sick, and you looked after me, I was in prison, and you came to visit me." Then the righteous will answer him, 'Lord, when did we see you hungry and feed you, or thirsty and give you something to drink? When did we see you a stranger and invite you in, or needing clothes and clothe you? When did we see you sick or in prison and go to visit you?' "The King will reply, 'Truly I tell you, whatever you did for one of the least of these brothers and sisters of mine, you did for me."

REFLECTION:

In Matthew 25:35-40, Jesus speaks about the importance of caring for those in need. He emphasises the need to feed the hungry, give drink to the thirsty, welcome the stranger, clothe the naked, and visit the sick and imprisoned. Jesus identifies himself with those in need, saying that when we care for them, we are caring for Him. This passage calls us to have a heart of compassion and to actively serve and care for those around us who are in need.

DECLARATION:

I declare that I will actively seek out opportunities to serve and care for those in need around me. I will seek to feed the hungry, give drink to the thirsty, welcome the stranger, clothe the naked, and visit the sick and imprisoned. I will do so with a heart of compassion, seeing Jesus in those I am serving. I will not turn a blind eye to the needs of those around me, but rather, I will be intentional in seeking ways to care for them.

MOTIVATION:

The motivation to care for those in need comes from the love of Christ within me. As Jesus identified Himself with those in need, I am motivated to serve and care for others with the same love and compassion that He showed. Additionally, I am motivated by the promise that when I serve others, I am serving Jesus himself. The desire to make a positive difference in the lives of those around me is a powerful motivation to actively seek out ways to care for them.

PRAYER:

Dear God, thank You for the opportunity to serve and care for those in need. Help me to have a heart of compassion, seeing Jesus in those I am serving. Show me the ways in which I can make a positive difference in the lives of those around me. I pray that You would give me the strength and wisdom to actively seek out opportunities to care for those in need. May my actions reflect Your love and compassion, and may they bring glory to Your name. In Jesus' name, Amen.

Appreciation

My thanks in making this book goes to our son Bruce. He is a wonderful photographer, and he has shared his photos with me from his trip to Patagonia. The Photo below is of him.

He was raising money for St. Andrews Hospice in Airdrie. I will give the profits from this book to St. Andrews Hospice.

Thanks to Colin my husband and Michelle our daughter for all their support and help in editing.

Thanks also to Nikki Love who works with me. Nikki is a great support in suggestions and layouts etc.

About the author

Cindy has been blessed with doing many things in her life. I started out nursing and after hurting my back at work, We asked God to show us the next step for our lives.

Colin felt the time was right to leave church ministry and after much we felt guided to work with Belarus concentrating on children affected by the Chernobyl Disaster. We formed a Charity board called Servants Aloft Ministries. Sam for short. Everyone was a good help and support to us at that time.

There are so many stories perhaps I can do a book about that one day. My time over there meant we made so many friends and many people from Scotland came as well. Together it was like a family. My heart goes out to them still. We keep in touch and still help where we can.

The last 11 years I have been involved with Beauty Training and loved every minute. Seeing students coming in and feeling nervous and watching them as the penny drops and they can confidently start giving treatment by themselves is a pure joy for teachers. Through our schools we have given out over 8400 diplomas.

I started writing when I was 50 years old my first book was angel encounters. It has very personal stories of people who felt the presence of an Angel in very difficult situations. After that I was working on beauty manuals. I have written over 40 of them. Now as I am getting older my books are devoted to God. I hope this book Everlasting Love will help you to concentrate on what the bible is saying about God's love. This book can help you through difficult times as well as the happy ones.

For anyone reading it, thank you very much. I hope you can meditate not only on the words but through the photos as well.

In this book Gods tells us to strive to be the best,

No one is perfect but if we aim at nothing, we will achieve nothing. I am not the best example by far, but I aim to be the best with God's help. Every blessing Cindy.

You can see any future books coming out on Facebook just look for Cindy Mackenzie Ministries.

https://www.facebook.com/groups/20693735942 1178

For Bruce's photography in many areas, such as landscapes, weddings & events check out http://brucemackenziephotography.squarespac e.com

Colin my Husband has beautiful Vlogs of Scotland

www.youtube.com/@colinmackenziephotography9009.

Our daughter is also an author of children's book and in November her first novel Landis is being published with an American company

Monarch.

https://monarcheducationalservices.com/ We are all looking forward to this. She has worked hard. You can follow her at https://shellymackbooks.co.uk on Amazon.

Printed in Great Britain
by Amazon

27116619R00059